A Kid's Guide to Drawing America™

How to Draw
New Jersey's
Sights and Symbols

Melody S. Mis

The Rosen Publishing Group's
PowerKids Press™
New York

To Tyler Raben and Andrew Reilly

Published in 2002 by The Rosen Publishing Group, Inc.
29 East 21st Street, New York, NY 10010

First Edition

Editor: Jannell Khu
Book Design: Kim Sonsky
Layout Design: Colin Dizengoff

Illustration Credits: Laura Murawski except p. 27 by Emily Muschinske.
Photo Credits: p. 7 © Kelly-Mooney Photography/CORBIS; pp. 8, 9 © The Montclair Art Museum, Montclair, New Jersey; pp. 12, 14 © One Mile Up, Incorporated; p. 16 © Bill Ross/CORBIS; p. 18 © Chinch Gryniewicz; Ecoscene/CORBIS; p. 20 © James L. Amos/CORBIS; p. 22 © Larry Neubauer/CORBIS; p. 24 © Amos Nachoum/CORBIS; p. 26 courtesy of Jason Minick; p. 28 © Joseph Sohm; Visions of America/CORBIS.

Mis, Melody S.
How to draw New Jersey's sights and symbols / Melody S. Mis.
p. cm. — (A kid's guide to drawing America)
Includes index.
Summary: This book explains how to draw some of New Jersey's sights and symbols, including the state seal, the official flower, and the Barnegat lighthouse.
 ISBN 0-8239-6086-2
1. Emblems, State—New Jersey—Juvenile literature   2. New Jersey—In art—Juvenile literature   3. Drawing—Technique—Juvenile literature   [1. Emblems, State—New Jersey 2. New Jersey   3. Drawing—Technique]   I. Title   II. Series
 2001
 743'.8'99749—dc21
Manufactured in the United States of America

MOLLY PITCHER

CONTENTS

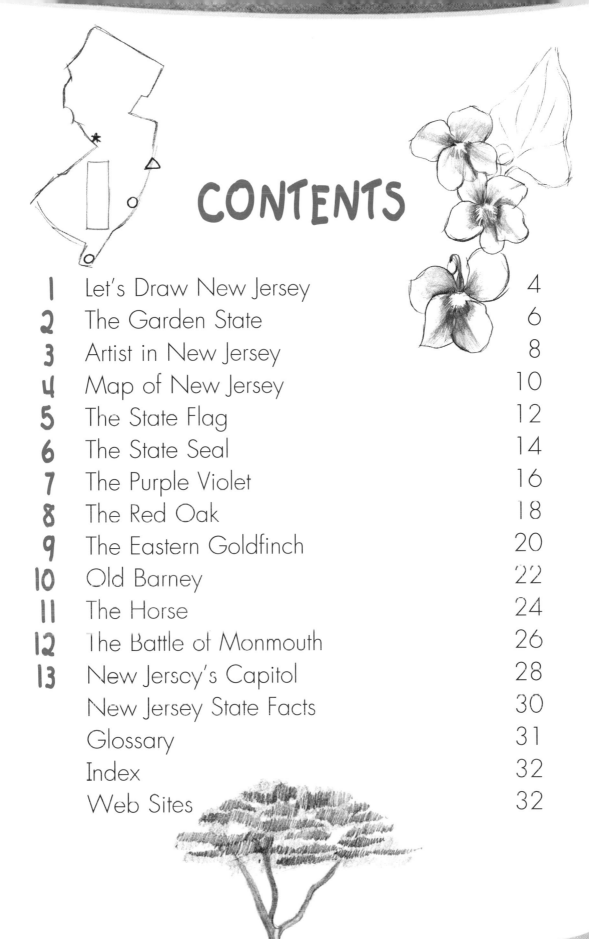

Let's Draw New Jersey

Early settlers in New Jersey farmed, mined, and logged for a living. In the 1800s, products and inventions in New Jersey helped the state become an industrial state. For example the Singer sewing machine, Band-Aid bandages, and Campbell soups were developed in New Jersey and strengthened the state's economy.

John Stevens is considered the father of American railroads. In 1825, he designed and built the first steam locomotive, an engine used to pull railroad cars, in Hoboken, New Jersey. Thomas Edison built a shop in Menlo Park, New Jersey, where he finalized his invention of the electric light bulb in 1879. Edison also invented the first motion-picture camera, called a kinetoscope, in 1889. With the kinetoscope, filmmaking became an important industry in New Jersey. Between 1903 and 1927, more than 900 films were made in Fort Lee, New Jersey! Movies filmed in New Jersey include *The Great Train Robbery*, and the series *Perils of Pauline*.

Today New Jersey leads the country in chemical

production for pharmaceutical and consumer products. Prescription medicine, shampoo, soap, and paint are just a few of the chemical products made in New Jersey.

New Jersey's sights and symbols are fun to draw, and this book will teach you how to draw some of them. You will start with simple shapes and will add other shapes to them. There are directions under each step. Each new step is in red to help guide you. Before you start, check out the drawing terms. You will need the following supplies to draw New Jersey's sights and symbols:

- A sketch pad
- An eraser

- A number 2 pencil
- A pencil sharpener

These are some of the shapes and drawing terms you'll need to know to draw New Jersey's sights and symbols:

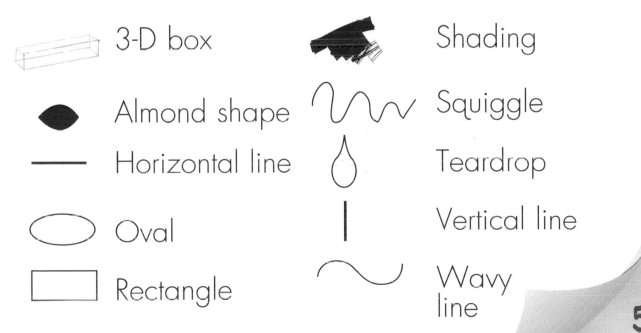

3-D box

Shading

Almond shape

Squiggle

Horizontal line

Teardrop

Oval

Vertical line

Rectangle

Wavy line

The Garden State

Early settlers nicknamed New Jersey the Garden State, because they supplied their neighboring colonies with the bounty of the state's crops. Today the Garden State lives up to the nickname with beautiful floral gardens. The Presby Memorial Iris Gardens in Upper Montclair have more than 4,000 varieties of irises! Leaming's Run Gardens and Colonial Farm in Swainton covers 30 acres (12 ha) and is the largest annual garden in the nation.

If you visit Atlantic City, New Jersey, you can take a stroll on the world's first boardwalk, built along Atlantic City's beach. Charles Darrow made the streets of Atlantic City famous when he used them in his game, Monopoly. You can also visit the site where the world's first complete dinosaur skeleton was found, near Haddonfield, in 1858. A trip to New Jersey wouldn't be complete without a visit to Six Flags Great Adventure. Located in Jackson, New Jersey, it is the largest theme park in the northeast.

Colorful autumn leaves cling to trees along cliffs in the New Jersey Palisades. Across the Hudson River is Bergen County, New Jersey.

Artist in New Jersey

George Inness

George Inness was one of America's most gifted landscape artists. He was born near Newburgh, New York, in 1825, and was raised in Newark, New Jersey.

When he first began to paint, Inness was influenced by the Hudson River school of landscape painting. The name Hudson River school comes from a group of painters in the nineteenth century. These artists depicted the wild, unsettled areas of the New York Hudson River Valley and the western frontier in a grand, dramatic way.

Although Inness began as a Hudson River school painter, he quickly developed his own painting style. He used softer lines and colors to paint landscapes than did the Hudson River school artists. Unlike most of the Hudson River school painters, many of Inness's landscapes included aspects of humankind. In fact Inness described his paintings as civilized landscapes. It was important to Inness to include a sense of civilization in his paintings.

Early Autumn, Montclair is a good example of Inness's painting style. In 1888, Inness captured the trees just as the leaves turned orange in early autumn. This painting is soft and hazy. This effect gives it a dreamlike quality. Inness left out details and sharpness in the painting to bring out the peaceful serenity of nature. Although people are not in the scene, he painted a building in the background to suggest the presence of people.

© The Montclair Art Museum, Montclair, NJ

Early Autumn, Montclair was done in oil on canvas and measures 30" x 45" (76 cm x 114 cm). During the last 20 years of his life, Inness kept art studios in Montclair, New Jersey, and New York City.

9

Map of New Jersey

Map of the Continental United States

The Hudson River, the Atlantic Ocean, and the Delaware River border New Jersey. The Delaware Water Gap, a deep gorge formed by erosion, and the Kittatinny Mountains are in northern New Jersey. New Jersey's tallest peak is High Point at 1,803 feet (549.5 m) above sea level. The Atlantic Coastal Plain borders the Atlantic Ocean. Some of the state's finest beach resorts, including Atlantic City and Cape May, are along the Atlantic Coastal Plain's seashore. Swamps, salt marshes, and pygmy pine trees are found in the New Jersey pinelands. The New Jersey Turnpike, a highway that runs through the state, links New York City to Philadelphia, Pennsylvania.

1

Study the shape before you begin to draw. The shape above consists of nine connected lines.

2

Use the red lines as guides to shape your map of New Jersey. Draw a five-pointed star for Trenton, the state capital.

3

Erase extra lines. Draw an open circle for Atlantic City. Atlantic City is located on the southeastern seashore of New Jersey.

4

Draw another open circle for Cape May. Fill in the circle. Place it at the southernmost part of the state.

5

Draw an open triangle for Island Beach State Park. Place it north of Atlantic City.

6

Draw a long rectangle for the Pine Barrens. You can also draw the map key.

The State Flag

During the American Revolution (1775–1783), each colony's regiment of the Continental army carried a flag. As commander of the Continental army, General George Washington selected different background colors for the flags of these regiments. He picked buff, which is a beige color, for New Jersey's flag. He chose buff to honor the Dutch settlers of New Jersey, who originally came from the Netherlands. Buff and dark blue are the colors of the Netherlands's insignia. An insignia is a badge of authority or of honor. In the center of the flag is the state seal. The seal was designed by Pierre Eugene du Simitiere, who also helped design the seal of the United States. New Jersey officially adopted this state flag in 1896.

1

Draw a rectangle.

2

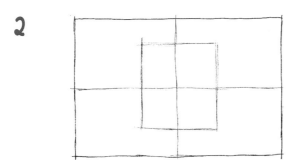

Through the middle of the rectangle, draw a horizontal line and a vertical line. Now draw a square in the middle of these two lines.

3

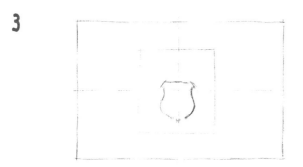

Draw the shape of the shield as shown. Notice how it's placed toward the bottom center of the square.

4

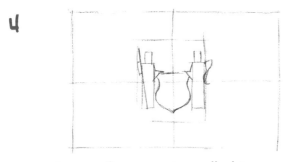

Draw the two figures using tall, thin rectangles for the bodies. Draw little rectangles for the heads and the arms.

5

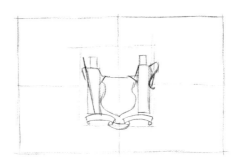

Now draw the wavy ribbon under the shield.

6

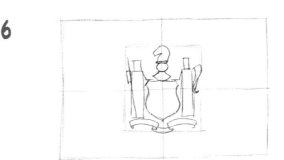

Draw a diamond, then a circle, and lastly, a horse's head.

7

Draw the curly branches next to the horse's head.

8

Erase the guidelines. Shape the heads of the figures into ovals and add details to their dresses. Draw the lines on the shield. Draw the horse's mane.

The State Seal

New Jersey's state seal was designed in 1777. In the center of the seal is a blue shield with three plows to symbolize the state's agriculture. On top of the shield is a helmet, which represents New Jersey's independence from Great Britain. Above the helmet is a horse's head. The horse stands for speed and strength. Lady Liberty is on the left of the shield, and she holds a staff with a red liberty cap on top of it. She stands for freedom. On the right of the shield is Ceres, the Roman goddess of agriculture. She holds a horn filled with fruits and vegetables. This symbolizes the abundance of food. The two women stand on a ribbon that has the state's motto, Liberty And Prosperity, written on it. Also written in the ribbon is 1776, the year that New Jersey wrote its first state constitution.

1

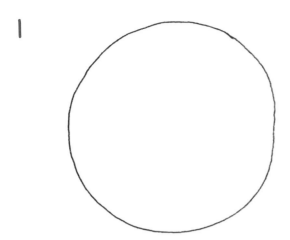

Draw a circle.

2

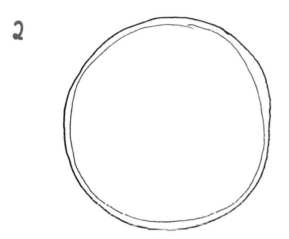

Draw another circle inside the first one you drew.

3

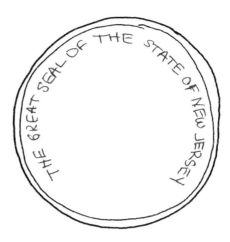

Write the words "THE GREAT SEAL OF THE STATE OF NEW JERSEY" inside the inner circle.

4

Inside the inner circle, draw the picture from the flag chapter. Now write "LIBERTY AND PROSPERITY" inside the ribbon. Notice that the date 1776 is in the center of the ribbon. Great job!

The Purple Violet

Violets are among the most popular state flowers. Various species of the flower have been adopted as the official flowers of Rhode Island, Wisconsin, and Illinois. The violet species adopted by New Jersey is the purple violet (*Viola sororia*). The purple violet became the official state flower of New Jersey in 1971.

The purple violet is a small flower that grows in the spring. Violets grow well in warm sunshine. Some of the flowers are deep purple, and some are white with purple speckles on them. These violets are called freckles! Violets are sometimes eaten in salads or are made into jelly.

1

Begin with three circles. Each circle is the basic shape of a violet.

2

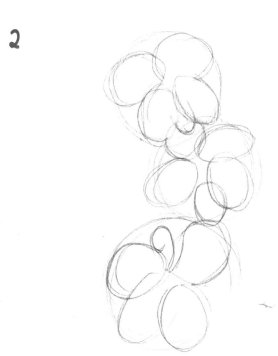

Draw loose circles and ovals for the petals. There are five petals in each flower.

3

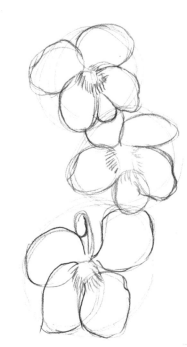

Go back over the petal shapes and make them more defined. Draw little details in the center of each flower.

4

Draw a leaf on the top right. Lightly draw five lines for the leaf veins. Erase extra lines. Turn your pencil on its side, and shade the petals. Notice how the shading is darkest in the center. Nice job!

The Red Oak

The red oak (*Quercus rubra Linn*) was adopted as New Jersey's state tree in 1950. The red oak gets its name from the tree's leaves. They turn red in the autumn. It can grow to be 90 feet (27 m) tall. Its branches provide a lot of shade on hot days, and its acorns provide food for animals. The red oak grows well in various types of soil. It can be found from Maine to Georgia, and from the Atlantic Coast to Minnesota. Since the 1600s, red oak trees from New Jersey have provided lumber for houses, wagons, and ships. Today red oak trees from New Jersey supply lumber for furniture and flooring in houses. The oldest oak tree is in Salem, New Jersey. According to scientists, it is more than 400 years old!

1

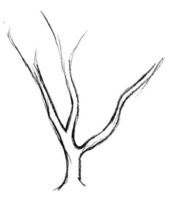

Draw the trunk and the branches with wavy lines. There are five main branches on this tree.

2

Turn your pencil on its side, and lightly shade the area on top of the trunk with short up-and-down strokes.

3

Continue to shade the tree. Press harder on your pencil. These are the leaves.

4

Now shade the trunk, and you are done!

The Eastern Goldfinch

The eastern goldfinch was adopted as New Jersey's state bird in 1935. This bird is so small, it can fit in your hand! The eastern goldfinch is about 5 inches (13 cm) long. The male goldfinch is easy to see, because his colors are bright. His body is yellow and his wings and head are black. The female goldfinch is a greenish brown color, the same color as her nest in the tree branches. Her color camouflages her and makes it hard for her enemies to see her and her babies when they are in the nest. The goldfinch is a songbird and makes a sound like "per-chic-o-ree." The goldfinch is an active bird that needs a lot of food. Insects and seeds are favorite meals of the eastern goldfinch.

1

Draw a circle. This is the head. Draw an oval on top of the circle. This is the body. Notice that the two shapes overlap.

2

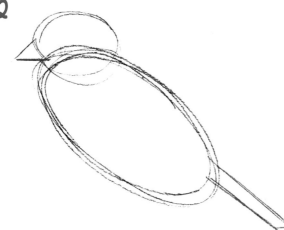

Draw a triangle for the beak. Draw a thin rectangle underneath the oval for the tail.

3

Connect the head to the body. Now draw a line from the tail to the body. Draw the bird's legs and its claws. Draw the bird's perch using two straight lines.

4

Now draw a little circle in the head for the eye. Draw a line in the triangle to make the beak. Add a line for the wing as shown. Erase extra lines.

5

Turn your pencil on its side, and gently shade the entire bird. Use the step above as a guide, and shade some areas darker than others. You can also smudge the bird with your finger.

Old Barney

Lighthouses were built on America's coastlines in the 1700s and the 1800s to warn ships of shallow and dangerous waters. Their lights guided ships safely into harbors. The Barnegat Lighthouse was designed by General George Meade and was built in 1858. Located on Long Beach Island, New Jersey, the Barnegat Lighthouse marks the area where more than 200 ships ran aground in shallow waters. Sailors nicknamed the lighthouse Old Barney. Its light could be seen from 30 miles (48 km) away. It is 165 feet (50 m) high and is the tallest lighthouse in New Jersey. You can climb up the 217 steps to the tower and can look at the Atlantic Ocean. Old Barney now serves as a museum. It is no longer used as a lighthouse.

1

Draw a long, thin rectangular shape that gets thinner toward the top.

2

To draw the top of the lighthouse, first outline the top. Then draw two horizontal lines under it. Next connect those lines with two vertical lines. Now draw two lines on the lighthouse. Notice the placement of these lines.

3

Inside the highest part of the lighthouse, draw five short, vertical lines and one horizontal line. Under it draw three vertical lines.

4

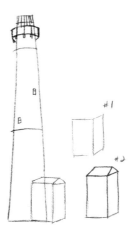

Now add the two windows. To draw the little building, look at guide #1 and then guide #2. This is a 3-D shape. You can practice on a piece of scratch paper.

5

Shade your drawing gradually. Turn your pencil on its side and gently stroke the paper. The lower part of the lighthouse should be lighter than the upper part.

The Horse

Horses are so popular in New Jersey that on August 14, 1977, the horse was chosen as the state's animal. Fifth graders from Our Lady of Victories in Harrington Park, New Jersey, created a petition to make this happen! Horses have roamed the earth for nearly three million years. Horses were one of the most important animals to be domesticated. They were used for transportation, pulling heavy equipment, and plowing farm fields.

Today many people in New Jersey enjoy equestrian activities, including riding and racing horses. The Horse Park of New Jersey, the state's first horse show grounds, is located in Monmouth County. Monmouth has more horses than does any other New Jersey county.

1

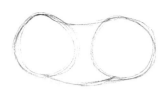

Draw two circles. Connect the circles with curved lines as shown. This is the body of the horse.

2

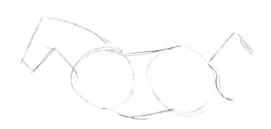

Five lines make up the horse's head and neck. Start with the curved line on top, and then draw the three lines that make up its face. Finish with the line that will be its neck. For its tail, draw two straight lines and one curved line.

3

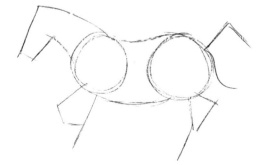

Draw the bent front leg first. It consists of three lines. The other front leg is easy to draw. Simply draw a slanted, straight line. Both hind legs consist of two bent lines.

4

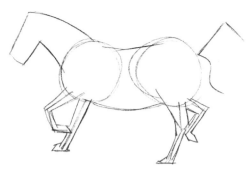

Use the lines you drew in the previous step as guides to finish the legs and the hooves.

5

Use the red highlighted lines as guides to soften your horse drawing. Add the ear, the eye, the nostril, and the mouth. Erase extra lines.

6

Shade the horse. Pay careful attention to the horse's tail when you shade. Good work!

The Battle of Monmouth

The Battle of Monmouth in Freehold, New Jersey, was one of the major battles of the American Revolution. It was fought on June 28, 1778, and neither the British nor the Americans won. It took five more years before the thirteen colonies defeated the British and gained independence.

A brave woman became a legend at the Battle of Monmouth. Her name was Mary Ludwig Hays. Her husband was a soldier in General George Washington's army. According to legend, Mary took pitchers of water to the tired, thirsty soldiers in the battlefield at the Battle of Monmouth. She even fired a cannon! The soldiers gave her the nickname Molly Pitcher.

1

Draw the head first. Carefully draw one line at a time. First draw a vertical line under the oval. Draw a horizontal line for the shoulder. For the hips, draw a slightly slanted, shorter line. Draw the lines that make up her legs and feet. Lastly, draw the arms.

2

Draw two short lines for Molly's neck. Draw four small circles for the collar. To draw the vest, follow the red highlighted lines. Draw details like the vest V neckline and the belt.

3

Fill in Molly's arms using the lines you drew as a guide. Her upper arms are puffy because of her clothes.

4

Copy the red highlighted lines to draw Molly's skirt. It consists of three lines.

5

Draw Molly's boots. They have square heels.

6

Erase extra lines so that your drawing looks like the above. Add the tool she holds in her hands.

7

Draw Molly's face and hair. Shade the tool. Now draw a shadow underneath Molly.

8

Shade your drawing. Notice the shadows in Molly's skirt. Draw Molly's platform and write "MOLLY PITCHER" on it.

New Jersey's Capitol

Today gold sparkles on the dome of New Jersey's historic statehouse. The capitol, designed by Jonathan Doane, was built in Trenton in 1792. The building did not have a dome when it was built. The dome was added in 1845. Years later, during the cold winter of 1885, fire destroyed some parts of the capitol, including the rotunda and the dome. Firefighters had a difficult time controlling the fire, because the water supply was frozen. After the fire, Lewis Broome, from Jersey City, was selected to rebuild the capitol. He designed the new rotunda with its gold dome. To apply gold leaf to the dome, workers had to flatten the gold into sheets. It took 1 ½ miles (2 km) of these gold sheets to finish the beautiful dome.

1

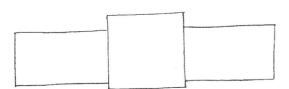

Draw a square. Draw a rectangle on the right side of the square and another one on the left. Make the rectangles shorter than the square.

2

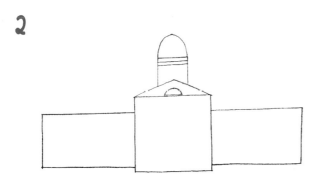

Draw two slanted lines that meet at a point on top of the square. Draw a half circle inside these two slanted lines. On top of the two slanted lines, draw a long, curved dome shape. Draw three horizontal lines inside this dome shape.

3

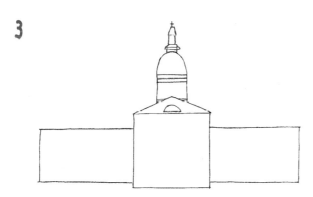

Draw two more lines on the dome, behind the triangle shape. Draw the shapes on top of the dome as shown. Start with the bottom shape, and then draw your way up. Finish with the cross.

4

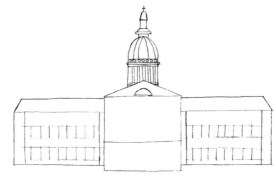

Draw lines in the dome. Add little circles underneath. For the columns, draw vertical lines underneath the dome. Draw horizontal and vertical lines in the rectangles. These are the windows. Draw a horizontal line across the square.

5

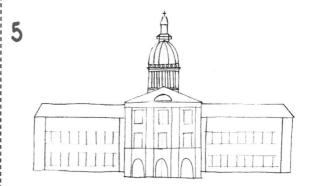

Draw vertical lines in the square. Draw six little boxes for the windows. Draw three half ovals underneath the windows.

6

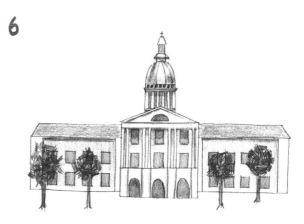

Shade the drawing. Turn your pencil on its side, and shade lightly. Notice that the windows and the spaces between the columns are dark.

New Jersey State Facts

Statehood	December 18, 1787, 3rd state
Area	8,215 square miles (21,277 sq km)
Population	8,414,400
Capital	Trenton, population, 85,400
Most Populated City	Newark, population, 268,500
Industries	Chemicals, tourism, pharmaceuticals
Agriculture	Fruits, vegetables, dairy
Animal	Horse
Dance	Square dance
Bird	Eastern goldfinch
Flower	Purple violet
Fish	Brook trout
Fossil	*Hadrosaurus foulkii* (dinosaur)
Tree	Red oak
Insect	Honeybee
Shell	Knobbed whelk
Colors	Buff and blue
Motto	Liberty And Prosperity
Nickname	The Garden State

Glossary

abundance (uh-BUN-dents) More than enough, plentiful.

American Revolution (uh-MER-uh-ken reh-vuh-LOO-shun) Battles that soldiers from the American colonies fought against England for freedom.

aspect (AS-pehkt) A particular feature or characteristic of something.

boardwalk (BORD-wok) A walkway made of wooden boards, generally at a beach.

camouflages (KAH-muh-fla-jihz) Disguises to look like the surroundings.

civilized (SIH-vuhl-yzd) A condition of human society.

Continental army (kon-tin-EN-tul AR-mee) The army of patriots created in 1775 with George Washington as its commander in chief.

domesticated (duh-MES-tih-kayt-id) To have tamed a wild animal for human use.

dramatic (druh-MAH-tik) Striking in appearance and effect.

equestrian (ih-kwes-tree-un) Having to do with riding horses.

erosion (ih-ROH-zhun) To be worn away slowly.

gorge (GORJ) A steep, narrow passage through land.

hazy (HAY-zee) Unclear or blurred.

independence (in-dih-PEN-dints) Freedom from the control of others.

legend (LEH-jind) A story passed down through the years.

marshes (MARSH-ez) Areas of wet land.

petition (peh-TIH-shun) A formal written request.

pharmaceutical (far-muh-SOO-tih-kul) Pertaining to drugs and drugstores.

prescription medicines (pri-SKRIP-shun MED-uh-sinz) The type and amount of drugs doctors order for patients who are sick.

prosperity (pros-PAIR-uh-tee) Success.

pygmy (PIHG-mee) Small, dwarfish.

regiment (REH-jih-ment) A group of soldiers.

rotunda (roh-TUN-dah) A round dome.

serenity (seh-REH-nih-tee) Calm and peaceful.

Index

A
American Revolution, 12, 26
Atlantic City, 6, 10

B
Barnegat Lighthouse, 23
Battle of Monmouth, 26

C
Cape May, 10
capitol, 28

D
Delaware Water Gap, 10

E
Edison, Thomas, 4

H
Horse Park of New Jersey, 24
Hudson River school, 8

I
Inness, George, 8–9

N
Netherlands, the, 12

P
Pitcher, Molly, 26
prescription medicine, 5

R
red oak, 18

S
Six Flags Great Adventure, 6
state bird, 20
state flag, 12, 14
state flower, 16
state seal, 12

T
Trenton, New Jersey, 28

Web Sites

To learn more about New Jersey, check out these Web sites:
http://www.visitnj.com
http://www.nj.us